WITHDRAWN **of alcohol-and drug-related issues in the workplace**

Two week loan

Please return on or before the last date stamped below.
Charges are made for late return.

CANCELLED		
CANCELLED		
CANCELLED		
CANCELLED		

An ILO code of practice

Management of alcohol- and drug-related issues in the workplace

International Labour Office   Geneva

ILO
Management of alcohol- and drug-related issues in the workplace. An ILO code of practice
Geneva, International Labour Office, 1996

/Code of practice/, /Drug abuse/, /Alcoholism/, /Occupational health/,
/Personnel management/. 13.04.7
ISBN 92-2-109455-3

Also published in French: *Prise en charge des questions d'alcoolisme et de toxicomanie sur le lieu de travail.* Recueil de directives pratiques (ISBN 92-2-209455-7), Geneva, 1996

In Spanish: *Tratamiento de cuestiones relacionadas con el alcohol y las drogas en el lugar de trabajo.* Repertorio de recomendaciones prácticas de la OIT (ISBN 92-2-309455-0), Geneva, 1996

ILO Cataloguing in Publication Data

Printed in Switzerland ATA

Preface

Problems relating to alcohol and drugs may arise as a consequence of personal, family or social factors, or from certain work situations, or from a combination of these elements. Such problems not only have an adverse effect on the health and well-being of workers, but may also cause many work-related problems including a deterioration in job performance. Given that there are multiple causes of alcohol- and drug-related problems, there are consequently multiple approaches to prevention, assistance, treatment and rehabilitation.

While the elimination of substance abuse is a highly desirable goal, experience has shown the difficulty of achieving this. However, workplace policies to assist individuals with alcohol- and drug-related problems, including the use of illegal drugs, would seem to yield the most constructive results for workers and employers alike.

It was for this reason that the Governing Body of the ILO decided at its 259th Session (March 1994) to convene a meeting of experts in Geneva from 23 to 31 January 1995, to consider a draft code of practice on the management of alcohol- and drug-related problems at the workplace. The meeting was composed of seven experts appointed following consultations with governments, seven following consultations with the Employers' group, and seven following consultations with the Workers' group of the Governing Body.[1]

---

[1] *Experts appointed following consultations with governments:*

Ms. Eslahe Mohamed Amin, Director-General, Department of International Workers' Relations, Ministry of Manpower and Employment, Cairo (Egypt).

Mr. Anatoli V. Chevtchenko, Chief Specialist on Narcology, Ministry of Health and Medical Industry of the Russian Federation, Moscow (Russian Federation).

Mr. Juarez Corréia Barros, Jr., Occupational Safety Engineer, Regional Labour Commission of the State of São Paulo (DRT/SP), São Paulo (Brazil).

The practical recommendations of this code of practice are intended to provide guidance to all those who have responsibility for addressing alcohol- and drug-related problems at the workplace. The code is not intended to replace international standards, national laws, regulations or other accepted standards. Alcohol and drug policies and programmes should apply to all staff, managers and employees and should not discriminate on grounds of race, colour, sex, religion, political opinion, national extraction or social origin.

The following constitute the key points in this code of practice:

– Alcohol and drug policies and programmes should promote the prevention, reduction and management of alcohol- and drug-related problems in the workplace. This code applies to all types of public and private employment including the informal sector. Legislation and national policy in this field should be determined after consultation with the most representative employers' and workers' organizations.

————

Ms. Dorothy Dzvova, National Coordinator, Department of Social Welfare, Ministry of Labour, Harare (Zimbabwe).

Mr. Georg Kleinsorge, Advisor, Ministry of Labour, Bonn (Germany).

Ms. Judith Peterson, Substance Abuse Program Coordinator, US Department of Labor, Washington, DC (United States).

Mr. Wilhelm Soriano, Executive Director, Employees Compensation Commission, Manila (the Philippines).

Advisers: Mr. Naguib Gheita (Egypt). Mr. Herbert Ziegler (Germany).

Experts appointed following consultations with the Employers' group:

Mr. François Alric, Assistant to the Director-General, Inter Services Centre on Occupational Health and Medicine (CISME), Paris (France).

Mr. André Beugger, Group Personnel Manager, Chamber of Mines of South Africa, Johannesburg (South Africa).

Mr. Ramiro Castro de la Matta Caamaño, President of the Governing Council, Information and Education Centre for the Prevention of Drug Abuse (CEDRO), Lima (Peru).

- Alcohol- and drug-related problems should be considered as health problems, and therefore should be dealt with, without any discrimination, like any other health problem at work and covered by the health care systems (public or private) as appropriate.
- Employers and workers and their representatives should jointly assess the effects of alcohol and drug use in the workplace, and should cooperate in developing a written policy for the enterprise.
- Employers, in cooperation with workers and their representatives, should do what is reasonably practicable to identify job situations that contribute to alcohol- and drug-related problems, and take appropriate preventive or remedial action.
- The same restrictions or prohibitions with respect to alcohol should apply to both management personnel and workers, so that there is a clear and unambiguous policy.
- Information, education and training programmes concerning alcohol and drugs should be undertaken to promote safety and health in the workplace and should be integrated where feasible into broad-based health programmes.

Mr. Reylito A.H. Elbo, Personnel and Administration Manager, Directories Philippines Corporation, Manila (the Philippines).

Ms. Caroline Jenkinson, Head of Research and Information Unit, Irish Business and Employers Confederation (IBEC), Dublin (Ireland).

Mr. Jim Lawson, Associate Vice-President, Human Resources Division, Head Office, Toronto-Dominion Bank, Toronto (Canada).

Professor Muyunda Mwanalushi, Education Services, Zambia Consolidated Copper Mines Ltd., Kitwe (Zambia).

Experts appointed following consultation with the Workers' group:

Mr. Miguel Angel Castrillón Collazos, Secretary for Health, Safety and Social Welfare, Single Confederation of Workers of Colombia (CUT), Bogota (Colombia).

Mr. Thomas Freden, Ombudsman, Swedish Trade Union Confederation (LO), Stockholm (Sweden).

- Employers should establish a system to ensure the confidentiality of all information communicated to them concerning alcohol- and drug-related problems. Workers should be informed of exceptions to confidentiality which arise from legal, professional or ethical principles.

- Testing of bodily samples for alcohol and drugs in the context of employment involves moral, ethical and legal issues of fundamental importance, requiring a determination of when it is fair and appropriate to conduct such testing.

- The stability which ensues from holding a job is frequently an important factor in facilitating recovery from alcohol- and drug-related problems. Therefore, the social partners should acknowledge the special role the workplace may play in assisting individuals with such problems.

- Workers who seek treatment and rehabilitation for alcohol- or drug-related problems should not be discriminated against by the employer and should enjoy normal job security and the

---

Ms. Mary Lehman-MacDonald, Substance Abuse Specialist, AFL-CIO, Washington, DC (United States).

Mr. Nathan Liepchitz, Collaborator, National Office, General Confederation of Labour (CGT), Montreuil (France).

Mr. Thomas Mellish, Policy Officer, Organization and Services Department, Trades Union Congress (TUC), London (United Kingdom).

Mr. Mike Sheridan, Representative — Prairie Region, Canadian Labour Congress, Saskatoon (Canada).

Mr. Joseph Strachan, President, Trade Federation on Drugs, Chemicals, Petroleum and Allied Services, Federation of Free Workers, Manila (the Philippines).

Observers:

European Union.

International Confederation of Free Trade Unions.

International Council on Alcohol and Addictions.

International Council of Nurses.

International Organization of Employers.

World Health Organization.

same opportunities for transfer and advancement as their colleagues.

–   It should be recognized that the employer has authority to discipline workers for employment-related misconduct associated with alcohol and drugs. However, counselling, treatment and rehabilitation should be preferred to disciplinary action. Should a worker fail to cooperate fully with the treatment programme, the employer may take disciplinary action as considered appropriate.

–   The employer should adopt the principle of non-discrimination in employment based on previous or current use of alcohol or drugs, in accordance with national law and regulations.

Local circumstances, particularly legal and cultural attitudes towards alcohol and drug use, as well as financial and technical resources, will determine how far it is practicable to follow the provisions of this code. This code should also be read in the context of the conditions in the country proposing to use these recommendations. With this in mind, the needs of developing countries have been taken into consideration.

The text of this code was approved for publication by the Governing Body of the ILO at its 262nd Session (March-April 1995).

World Federation of Trade Unions.

World Labour Confederation.

ILO representatives:

Mr. Joachim Reichling, Director, Training Department.

Mr. Willi Momm, Chief, Vocational Rehabilitation Branch, Training Department.

Mr. Behrouz Shahandeh, Senior Advisor on Drugs and Alcohol, Vocational Rehabilitation Branch, Training Department.

ILO consultants:

Dr. Sverre Fauske, International Project Coordinator.

Mr. Robert Husbands, Consultant.

Mr. Alan Le Serve, Consultant.

Contents

Appendices

1. General provisions

1.1. Objectives

1.1.1. The objectives of this code are to promote the prevention, reduction and management of alcohol- and drug-related problems in the workplace. In seeking to achieve this, the code provides guidance on:

(a) safeguarding the health and safety of all workers;

(b) preventing accidents;

(c) improving productivity and efficiency in the enterprise;

(d) promoting local, regional and national action to reduce the abuse of alcohol and drugs in the workplace;

(e) initiating and supporting programmes at the level of the workplace to assist those who are experiencing alcohol- or drug-related problems, or identifying workplace conditions which expose workers to a heightened risk of developing such problems;

(f) setting up an administrative, legal and educational framework within which preventive and remedial measures concerning alcohol- and drug-related problems can be designed and implemented, including measures to protect the confidentiality, privacy and dignity of workers;

(g) promoting consultation and cooperation between governments, employers, workers and their representatives, with the assistance of safety personnel, occupational health personnel, medical personnel and specialists in alcohol- and drug-related problems.

1.2. Application and uses

1.2.1. This code applies to all types of public and private employment.

1.2.2. The provisions of this code should be considered as basic recommendations and practical guidance for preventing, reducing and managing alcohol- and drug-related problems in the workplace. However, more protective national or international standards or regulations, as well as more protective collective agreements, would override the provisions of this code.

1.3. Definitions[1]

1.3.1. In this code, the following terms have the meanings hereby assigned to them:

Abuse (drug, alcohol, chemical, substance, or psychoactive substance): A group of terms in wide use but of varying meaning. In DSM-IIIR,[2] "psychoactive substance abuse" is defined as "a maladaptive pattern of use indicated by ... continued use despite knowledge of having a persistent or recurrent social, occupational, psychological or physical problem that is caused or exacerbated by the use [or by] recurrent use in situations in which it is physically hazardous". It is a residual category, with "dependence" taking precedence when applicable. The term "abuse" is sometimes used disapprovingly to refer to any use at all, particularly of illicit drugs. Because of its ambiguity, the term is not used in ICD-10 (except in the case of non-dependence-producing substances ...); "harmful use" and "hazardous use" are the equivalent terms in WHO usage, although they usually relate only to effects on health and not to social consequences.

---

[1] These definitions are largely drawn from the following publications: *Lexicon of alcohol and drug terms*, Geneva, World Health Organization, 1994; "Health promotion in the workplace: Alcohol and drug abuse", report of a WHO Expert Committee, Geneva, World Health Organization, 1993 (WHO Technical Report Series, No. 833). Some definitions were drawn from instruments and publications of the International Labour Organization.

[2] *Diagnostic and statistical manual of mental disorders*, 3rd ed. (revised), Washington, DC, American Psychiatric Association, 1987 (DSM-IIIR).

"Abuse" is also discouraged by the Office of Substance Abuse Prevention in the United States, although terms such as "substance abuse" remain in wide use in North America to refer generally to problems of psychoactive substance use.

In other contexts, abuse has referred to non-medical or unsanctioned patterns of use, irrespective of consequences. Thus the definition published in 1969 by the WHO Expert Committee on Drug Dependence was "persistent or sporadic excessive drug use inconsistent with or unrelated to acceptable medical practice".

After-care: The provision of services to persons in the period after formal counselling, treatment and rehabilitation, in order to assist them during a period of adjustment to independent functioning within the community.

Alcohol: In chemical terminology, alcohols are a large group of organic compounds derived from hydrocarbons and containing one or more hydroxyl (-OH) groups. Ethanol (C_2H_5OH, ethyl alcohol) is one of this class of compounds, and is the main psychoactive ingredient in alcoholic beverages. By extension the term "alcohol" is also used to refer to alcoholic beverages.

Ethanol results from the fermentation of sugar by yeast. Under usual conditions, beverages produced by fermentation have an alcohol concentration of no more than 14 per cent. In the production of spirits by distillation, ethanol is boiled out of the fermented mixture and recollected as an almost pure condensate. Apart from its use for human consumption, ethanol is used as a fuel, as a solvent, and in chemical manufacturing.

Absolute alcohol (anhydrous ethanol) refers to ethanol containing not more than 1 per cent by mass of water. In statistics on alcohol production or consumption, absolute alcohol refers to the alcohol content (as 100 per cent ethanol) of alcoholic beverages.

Methanol (CH_3OH), also known as methyl alcohol and wood alcohol, is chemically the simplest of the alcohols. It is used as an industrial solvent and also as an adulterant to denature ethanol and make it unfit to drink (methylated spirits). Methanol is highly toxic; depending on the amount consumed, it may produce blurring of vision, blindness, coma, and death.

Other non-beverage alcohols that are occasionally consumed, with potentially harmful effects, are isopropanol (isopropyl alcohol, often in rubbing alcohol) and ethylene glycol (used as antifreeze for automobiles).

Alcohol is a sedative/hypnotic with effects similar to those of barbiturates. Apart from social effects of use, alcohol intoxication may result in poisoning or even death; long-term heavy use may result in dependence or in a wide variety of physical and organic mental disorders.

Alcohol-related mental and behavioural disorders are classified as psychoactive substance use disorders in ICD-10.[1]

Alcohol and drug dependence: As a general term, the state of needing or depending on something or someone for support or to function or survive. As applied to alcohol and other drugs, the term implies a need for repeated doses of the drug to feel good or to avoid feeling bad. In DSM-IIIR, dependence is defined as "a cluster of cognitive, behavioural and physiologic symptoms that indicate a person has impaired control of psychoactive substance use and continues use of the substance despite adverse consequences".

---

[1] *International statistical classification of diseases and related health problems. Tenth revision. Vol. 1: Tabular list.* Geneva, World Health Organization, 1992 (ICD-10).

Alcohol- and drug-related problems: The term "alcohol- and drug-related problems" can be applied to any of the range of adverse accompaniments of drinking or drug-taking. It is important to note that "related" does not necessarily imply causality. The term can be used either of an individual drinker or drug user or at the level of society as a whole. It may be taken to include both dependence and abuse, but it also covers other problems.

Community-based institutions: Organizations of a non-medical or medical character that assist individuals with alcohol- and drug-related problems. Examples of such organizations are Alcoholics Anonymous (AA); Narcotics Anonymous (NA); governmental or non-governmental agencies or offices providing assistance; community associations, clubs, fraternal organizations, religious organizations, or any other group or association which assists persons with alcohol- and drug-related problems.

Competent authority: A minister, government department, or other public authority with the power to issue regulations, orders or other instructions having the force of law.

Detoxification: The process by which an individual is withdrawn from the effects of a psychoactive substance.

Drug: A term of varied usage. In medicine, it refers to any substance with the potential to prevent or cure disease or enhance physical or mental welfare, and in pharmacology to any chemical agent that alters the biochemical or physiological processes of tissues or organisms. Hence, a drug is a substance that is, or could be, listed in a pharmacopoeia. In common usage, the term often refers specifically to psychoactive drugs, and often, even more specifically, to illicit drugs, of which there is non-medical use in addition to any medical use. Professional formulations (e.g. "alcohol and other drugs") often seek to make the point that caffeine, tobacco, alcohol and other substances in common non-medical use are also drugs in the sense of being taken at least in part for their psychoactive effects.[1]

Employee Assistance Programme (EAP): A programme – either operated by the employer and a workers' organization jointly – or the employer alone, or a workers' organization alone, that offers assistance to workers, and frequently also to their family members, who have problems that affect – or that eventually could affect – job performance. An EAP can provide assistance to those with alcohol- and drug-related problems; but in many cases it also offers assistance with other problems liable to cause personal distress, including marital or family difficulties, depression, on-the-job or off-the-job stress, financial problems, or legal difficulties.

Employer: Any physical or legal person who employs one or more workers.

Harmful use: A pattern of psychoactive substance use that is causing damage to health. The damage may be physical (e.g. hepatitis following injection of drugs) or mental (e.g. depressive episodes secondary to heavy alcohol intake). Harmful use commonly, but not invariably, has adverse social consequences; social consequences in themselves, however, are not sufficient to justify a diagnosis of harmful use.

The term was introduced in ICD-10 and supplanted "non-dependent use" as a diagnostic term. The closest equivalent in other diagnostic systems (e.g. DSM-IIIR) is substance abuse, which usually includes social consequences.

Impairment: Any loss or abnormality of a psychological, physiological or physical function.

---

[1] The use of tobacco is not within the subject-matter addressed by this code.

Intoxication: A condition that follows the administration of a psychoactive substance and results in disturbances in the level of consciousness, cognition, perception, judgement, affect, or behaviour, or other psychophysiological functions and responses. The disturbances are related to the acute pharmacological effects of, and learned responses to, the substance and resolve with time, with complete recovery, except where tissue damage or other complications have arisen.

Occupational health services (OHS): Health services which have essentially a preventive function, and which are responsible for advising the employer, as well as the workers and their representatives, on the requirements for establishing and maintaining a safe and healthy working environment to facilitate optimal physical and mental health in relation to work. The OHS also provide advice on the adaptation of work to the capabilities of workers in the light of their physical and mental health.

Psychoactive drug or substance: A substance that, when ingested, affects mental processes, e.g. cognition or affect. This term and its equivalent, psychotropic drug, are the most neutral and descriptive terms for the whole class of substances, licit and illicit, of interest to drug policy. "Psychoactive" does not necessarily imply dependence-producing, and in common parlance, the term is often left unstated, as in "drug abuse" or "substance abuse". (*See also* Drug.)

Workers' representatives: Persons who are recognized as such by national law or practice, in accordance with the Workers' Representatives Convention, 1971 (No. 135).

2. General duties, rights and responsibilities

2.1. General duties of competent authorities

2.1.1. Legislation and national policy with respect to the prevention, reduction and management of alcohol- and drug-related problems in the workplace should be determined after consultation with the most representative employers' and workers' organizations and other experts.

2.1.2. The competent authority should collect, maintain and publish statistics on accidents where use of alcohol or drugs has been determined to have been a factor.

2.1.3. Based on the conclusions of investigations and statistical data on accidents associated with the use of alcohol or drugs, the competent authority should take the following actions to prevent, reduce and manage such problems more effectively in the future:

(a) make appropriate recommendations for changes in the regulatory framework;

(b) offer technical information and advice to individual enterprises on ways to deal with such problems;

(c) issue monographs or other publications on ways to prevent accidents due to alcohol, legal and illegal drug use in the various industries, branches, production processes and occupational categories particularly at risk.

2.1.4. In regulations and legislation developed by the competent authority, alcohol- and drug-related problems should be considered as health problems, and therefore dealt with, without any discrimination, as any other health problem at work and covered by the health care systems (public or private) as appropriate and practicable. Counselling, treatment and rehabilitation are important elements in this context.

2.1.5. The competent authority should monitor the implementation of legislation and regulations applicable to alcohol and drugs in the workplace by, for example, carrying out inspections of the workplace, and take appropriate measures to ensure that such legislation and regulations are enforced.

2.1.6. The competent authority should supply technical information and advice to employers and workers concerning the most effective means of complying with legislation and regulations applicable to alcohol and drugs in the workplace.

2.2. General duties and rights of employers

2.2.1. Employers should provide and maintain a safe and healthy workplace in accordance with the applicable law and regulations, and take appropriate actions, including the adoption of a comprehensive workplace alcohol and drugs policy, to prevent accidents and safeguard the workers' health.

2.2.2. Employers should also strictly respect laws and regulations, in addition to those concerning occupational safety and health, which are applicable to alcohol and drugs in the workplace.

2.2.3. Employers should pursue good management practices, adopt fair employment practices, organize work in a satisfactory way and strive constantly to create a working environment that does not cause undue stress or physical or mental hardship.

2.2.4. Employers should take measures, e.g. information, education, training and the improvement of working conditions, to prevent alcohol- and drug-related problems from occurring in the workplace.

2.2.5. Employers should have the right to take appropriate measures with respect to workers with alcohol- and drug-related problems which affect, or which could reasonably be expected to affect, their work performance.

2.2.6. Employers should cooperate with law enforcement authorities if there are reasonable grounds to suspect that activities involving illegal drugs are taking place in the workplace. However, it should be recognized that employers are not equipped to be law enforcement agents and do not have training or qualifications in this area. Therefore, while employers, like other citizens, have a duty to cooperate with law enforcement authorities, they should not have an independent duty to act in the place of law enforcement agents or otherwise take steps to act on their behalf to enforce provisions under criminal law with respect to illegal drugs.

2.2.7. Employers should establish a system to maintain the confidentiality of all information communicated to them concerning alcohol- and drug-related problems. Workers should be informed of exceptions to confidentiality which arise from legal or professional ethical principles.

2.2.8. In the elaboration of directives and rules applicable to alcohol and drugs in the workplace, employers should consult and negotiate with workers and their representatives.

2.2.9. Employers should have access to the advice and services of competent professionals to advise them on the development and implementation of an alcohol and drug policy for the workplace, and employers should respect the integrity of such professionals.

2.3. General duties and rights of workers and their representatives

2.3.1. Workers and their representatives should respect all laws and regulations applicable to alcohol and drugs in the workplace.

2.3.2. Workers and their representatives should cooperate with the employer to prevent accidents at work due to harmful use of alcohol or abuse of drugs.

2.3.3. Workers and their representatives should cooperate with the employer to maintain safety and health in the workplace and bring to the attention of the employer conditions in the workplace that may encourage, incite, or lead to alcohol- and drug-related problems, and should suggest remedial measures.

2.3.4. Workers and their representatives should cooperate with the employer in the development of an alcohol and drug policy.

2.3.5. Workers and their representatives should follow the employer's directives and rules applicable to alcohol and drugs in the workplace, and actively participate in the development of such directives and rules through consultation and negotiation where required by law or collective agreement.

2.3.6. Workers and their representatives should cooperate and participate in alcohol and drug programmes offered by the employer for the benefit of the workers, and actively participate in the development of such programmes through consultation and negotiation where required by law or collective agreement.

2.3.7. Workers and their representatives should assist those with alcohol- or drug-related problems to obtain the assistance needed for rehabilitation.

2.3.8. Workers and their representatives should have the right to expect that their right to privacy be respected and that any intrusion into the private life of the worker regarding alcohol or drug use is limited, reasonable and justified.

2.3.9. Workers and their representatives should have access to the advice and services of competent professionals to advise them on the development and implementation of an alcohol and drug policy for the workplace, and workers and their representatives should respect the integrity of such professionals.

3. Development of an alcohol and drug policy for the workplace

3.1. Cooperation between the social partners

3.1.1. The employer should, in cooperation with the workers and their representatives, develop in writing the enterprise's policy on alcohol and drugs in the workplace. Where feasible, the development of such a policy should also be conducted in cooperation with medical personnel and other experts who have specialized knowledge regarding alcohol- and drug-related problems.

3.2. Contents of an alcohol and drug policy

3.2.1. A policy for the management of alcohol and drugs in the workplace should include information and procedures on:

(a) measures to reduce alcohol- and drug-related problems in the workplace through proper personnel management, good employment practices, improved working conditions, proper arrangement of work, and consultation between management and workers and their representatives;

(b) measures to prohibit or restrict the availability of alcohol and drugs in the workplace;

(c) prevention of alcohol- and drug-related problems in the workplace through information, education, training and any other relevant programmes;

(d) identification, assessment and referral of those who have alcohol- or drug-related problems;

(e) measures relating to intervention and treatment and rehabilitation of individuals with alcohol- or drug-related problems;

(f) rules governing conduct in the workplace relating to alcohol and drugs, the violation of which could result in the invoking of disciplinary procedures up to and including dismissal;

(g) equal opportunities for persons who have, or who have previously had, alcohol- and drug-related problems, in accordance with national laws and regulations.

3.3. Assessment

3.3.1. Employers and workers and their representatives should jointly assess the effects of alcohol and drug use in the workplace.

The following indicators, among others, should provide useful information for identifying and assessing the nature and size of the problem in a given enterprise:

(a) national and local surveys on prevalent consumption rates in the community;

(b) surveys which have been carried out in similar enterprises;

(c) absenteeism in terms of incidence of unauthorized leave and lateness;

(d) use of sick leave;

(e) accident rates;

(f) personnel turnover;

(g) alcohol consumption in the enterprise's canteen, cafeteria or dining area;

(h) opinions of supervisors and managers, workers and their representatives, safety personnel, and occupational health service personnel.

3.3.2. Although the above indicators can only give an approximate idea of the extent of alcohol- and drug-related problems collectively in the workplace, they should be useful in clarifying the enterprise's needs, target groups and priorities in the organization of prevention and assistance programmes. (See Appendix I concerning the development of an alcohol and drug programme for the workplace: elements of an alcohol and drug programme.)

4. Measures to reduce alcohol- and drug-related problems through good employment practices

4.1. Identification of working environment problems

4.1.1. Where it is indicated that certain job situations may contribute to alcohol- and drug-related problems, employers, in cooperation with workers and their representatives, should do what is reasonably practicable to identify and take appropriate preventive or remedial action. (See Appendix II.)

4.2. Corporate practices

4.2.1. Employers should not formally or informally support behaviour which incites, encourages or otherwise facilitates the harmful use of alcohol or the abuse of drugs on the premises.

4.2.2. Workers and their representatives should not formally or informally support behaviour which incites, encourages or otherwise facilitates the harmful use of alcohol or the abuse of drugs on the premises.

4.3. Job placement of rehabilitated workers

4.3.1. When a worker voluntarily discloses a previous history of alcohol- or drug-related problems to the employer, the employer should, where reasonably practicable, avoid exposing the rehabilitated individual to a working situation similar to that which, in the past, may have led to such problems.

5. Restrictions on alcohol, legal and illegal drugs in the workplace

5.1. Restrictions on alcohol

5.1.1. The employer or those persons otherwise responsible, after consultation with workers and their representatives, should consider restricting or prohibiting the possession, consumption and in sale of alcohol at the workplace, including the enterprise's canteen, cafeteria, and dining area.

5.1.2. The employer, after consultation with workers and their representatives, should consider withdrawing alcohol as an item for expense account reimbursement, or restricting it to well-defined situations and within certain well-defined limits of quantity of units consumed.

5.1.3. The employer should apply the same restrictions or prohibitions with respect to alcohol to both management personnel and workers, so that there is a clear and unambiguous policy.

5.1.4. The restrictions or prohibitions referred to above may vary significantly depending on the nature of the work and the national, cultural and social environment.

5.2. Availability of non-alcoholic beverages

5.2.1. The employer should ensure that non-alcoholic beverages, including water, are made available in locations where alcohol is available in the enterprise.

5.3. Restrictions on legal drugs

5.3.1. Where the use of medications may result in significant impairment, the individual should consult a qualified occupational health professional and give timely notice to the supervisor according to normal procedures for absence for health reasons. A qualified occupational health professional should then determine fitness for work with any necessary restrictions.

5.3.2. In countries where specific substances have been declared legal, the use of those substances at the workplace will be governed by the laws and regulations of those countries.

5.4. Restrictions on illegal drugs

5.4.1. In countries where specific substances have been declared illegal, the use of those substances at the workplace will be governed by the laws and regulations of those countries.

5.5. Payment in kind

5.5.1. The employer should be prohibited from paying any wages in the form of alcohol or drugs.

6. Prevention through information, education and training programmes

6.1. Effects of alcohol and drugs

6.1.1. Information, education and training programmes concerning alcohol and drugs should be undertaken to promote safety and health in the workplace either by the employer, the employer in cooperation with workers and their representatives, or by workers' organizations alone. Such programmes should be directed at all workers, and should contain information on the physical and psychological effects of alcohol and drug use (see Appendix III).

6.2. Information about the working environment

6.2.1. Information, education and training programmes concerning alcohol and drugs should include the following information with respect to the working environment and be directed at all workers:

(a) the laws and regulations covering alcohol and drugs which have general application, as well as those which are specific to the workplace;

(b) information pertaining to alcohol- and drug-related problems, provided, however, that individual confidentiality is respected;

(c) suggested measures to prevent such problems from occurring;

(d) services available to assist workers with alcohol- and drug-related problems, both within and outside of the enterprise, including information concerning assessment and referral services, counselling, treatment and rehabilitation programmes, as well as health insurance coverage for such services.

6.3. Training for supervisors and managers

6.3.1. In addition to participating in the information, education and training programmes that are directed at all workers, supervisory and managerial personnel should receive supplementary training to enable them:

(a) to identify changes in individual workplace performance and behaviour which may indicate that the services of an employee assistance programme (EAP) or health professional might be useful and give information on these services to the worker;

(b) to explain and respond to questions about the enterprise's policy regarding alcohol and drugs;

(c) to support a recovering worker's needs and monitor his or her performance, when the person returns to work;

(d) to assess the working environment and identify working methods or conditions which could be changed or improved to prevent, reduce or otherwise better manage alcohol- and drug-related problems.

6.4. Training for workers' representatives

6.4.1. In addition to becoming familiar with the information, education and training programmes that are directed at all workers, workers' representatives should receive supplementary training or be allowed facilities to conduct training to:

(a) refer workers who may need help to an employee assistance professional to identify signs and symptoms of potential alcohol- or drug-related problems;

(b) be able to assess the working environment and identify working methods or conditions which could be changed or improved to prevent, reduce or otherwise better manage alcohol- and drug-related problems;

(c) be able to explain and respond to questions about the enterprise's policy regarding alcohol and drugs;

(d) be able to help a rehabilitated worker with his or her needs when the person returns to work.

6.5. Delivery mechanisms

6.5.1. Information, education and training programmes about alcohol and drugs should be integrated where feasible into broad-based health programmes (see Appendix IV).

7. Identification

7.1. Different types of identification

7.1.1. The identification of individual workers with alcohol- or drug-related problems may be conducted at three levels:

(a) self-assessment by the worker, facilitated by information, education and training programmes;

(b) informal identification by friends, family members or colleagues, who suggest that the worker who appears to have a problem should seek assistance;

(c) formal identification by the employer, which may include testing.

7.2. Testing

7.2.1. Testing of bodily samples for alcohol and drugs in the context of employment involves moral, ethical and legal issues of fundamental importance, requiring a determination of when it is fair and appropriate to conduct such testing.

7.2.2. Testing should be undertaken in accordance with national laws and practice, which may vary considerably among member States.

7.2.3. An example of considerations to be taken into account in drug and alcohol testing is detailed in Appendix V – "Guiding principles on drug and alcohol testing in the workplace" adopted by the ILO Interregional Tripartite Experts Meeting on Drugs and Alcohol Testing in the Workplace, May 1993.

8. Assistance, treatment and rehabilitation programmes

8.1. Health character of alcohol- and drug-related problems

8.1.1. Workers with alcohol- or drug-related problems should be treated in the same way as workers with other health problems, in terms of benefits such as paid sick leave, paid annual leave, leave without pay and health-care insurance coverage, in accordance with national laws and regulations or as agreed upon in collective bargaining.

8.2. Job security and promotion

8.2.1. Workers who seek treatment and rehabilitation for alcohol- or drug-related problems should not be discriminated against by the employer and should enjoy normal job security and opportunity for transfer and advancement.

8.2.2. Exceptions to the principle of job security and promotion after the disclosure of alcohol- or drug-related problems by workers to their employer may be justified if the occupational health service (OHS) determines that an individual is no longer fit for a given job. In such circumstances, however, the employer should assist the worker to obtain access to counselling, treatment and rehabilitation.

8.3. Coordinating assistance to workers

8.3.1. Coordination of assistance by employers to workers who have alcohol- and drug-related problems will vary according to the size and nature of the enterprise, as well as according to national law, health-care and social security systems.

8.3.2. In the case of small enterprises, many of which do not have a health care unit and some of which do not have an organized framework for the representation of workers, employers should consider taking the following actions:

(a) identifying professionals and services which specialize in the counselling, treatment and rehabilitation of alcohol- and drug-related problems in the community and referring the worker to such professional assistance;

(b) identifying community-based organizations, including those of a medical and non-medical character, as well as self-help groups such as Alcoholics Anonymous (AA) and Narcotics Anonymous (NA), that may be useful to workers in dealing with their alcohol- or drug-related problems, and refer workers to such organizations;

(c) suggesting that the worker concerned contact his or her personal physician for initial assessment and treatment, and helping the worker locate a medical doctor if he or she does not have a personal physician.

8.3.3. In the case of enterprises which have an OHS unit, or have access to such services, the employer should refer workers who appear possibly to have alcohol- or drug-related problems to the OHS for assessment, initial counselling, treatment and rehabilitation, if this is within the competence of the health professionals engaged by the enterprise; the employer should refer workers to appropriate assistance outside the enterprise for counselling, treatment and rehabilitation that exceeds the competence of in-house health professionals.

8.3.4. Some employers may wish to consider the establishment of an Employee Assistance Programme (EAP), either as a joint programme in cooperation with the workers and/or with their representatives. Although employers normally have to have an enterprise of a certain size to support the cost of such a programme on an in-house basis, several small employers can support such programmes collectively, or contract for such services from an independent enterprise.

8.3.5. In some cases, workers and their representatives may also wish to establish their own assistance programmes alone and without the assistance of the employer, particularly when such programmes can service other workers in a particular or similar occupational category working for different employers; these worker-supported programmes are sometimes referred to as member assistance programmes.

8.3.6. Although EAPs may have different forms of organizations and services offered, they provide confidential assistance to workers – and frequently also their families – to help them with their alcohol- and drug-related problems and a whole range of other problems liable to cause personal distress, including marital or family difficulties, depression, anxiety or stress, financial problems or legal difficulties.

8.3.7. It is not the role of EAPs to determine fitness for work, which is a principal function of an OHS if one exists in a workplace, but rather to serve as a means of providing confidential assistance to workers, and frequently also to their families, in a neutral setting. In this regard, EAPs are sometimes located off-premises to enhance confidentiality. EAPs also normally engage in promotional activities to let workers know of the availability of the services offered, and sometimes engage in informational, educational and training activities for workers and supervisors.

8.3.8. EAPs may be organized in such a way that they act essentially as a point of initial assessment and referral to caregivers in the community, be they medical doctors, specialists in alcohol and drug counselling, treatment and rehabilitation, or community-based organizations, including those of a self-help character. Some EAPs, however, also engage appropriate personnel to provide actual counselling, treatment and rehabilitation services for individuals with alcohol- and drug-related problems, provided that referral to outside professionals or institutions is performed as necessary.

8.3.9. Counselling, treatment and rehabilitation programmes should be adapted to the individual needs of the person concerned.

8.4. Reintegration

8.4.1. After formal treatment, a recovery programme may include an ongoing period of after-care, which can be a crucial part of the assistance process.

8.4.2. When a qualified professional determines that a worker is successfully pursuing treatment, or has successfully completed treatment, the worker should, if feasible, be offered a transfer or retraining opportunity when the return to his or her previous occupational position is not appropriate.

8.4.3. During the period of a worker's reintegration, where recommended by the health-care provider, the employer should facilitate the worker's readaptation to the workplace.

8.5. Collective bargaining for treatment and rehabilitation benefits

8.5.1. To the extent that the costs of health care for alcohol- and drug-related problems are not covered by health care paid for by the State, or by the employer through employer-supported health care insurance, or paid for directly by the employer, workers and their representatives should consider negotiating for such treatment and rehabilitation benefits.

8.6. Privacy and confidentiality considerations

8.6.1. Any health-care providers employed by the enterprise should respect the principles of medical, psychological and counselling confidentiality and not disclose the person's condition, diagnosis or treatment to the employer. Occupational health personnel should be permitted to communicate to the employer whether a worker is fit or not, or fit with restrictions, and the duration of any disabling condition for health reasons, with regard to the performance of the person's job functions.

8.6.2. All records and information regarding alcohol- or drug-related problems disclosed voluntarily to the employer by the worker should be treated in the same way as other confidential health data. Such data should not be included in the worker's personnel file, and should be stored separately.

8.6.3. For practical reasons, disclosure by the worker of his or her condition to the supervisor may be advisable when in-patient or out-patient treatment is to take place. Disclosure in such circumstances should normally facilitate an understanding of the reasons for the worker's absence, and be taken into account and assist during his or her reintegration.

9. Intervention and disciplinary procedures

9.1. Preference for treatment to discipline

9.1.1. The employer should consider that workers who have problems with alcohol and drug use may be suffering from a health problem. In such circumstances, the employer should normally offer counselling, treatment and rehabilitation alternatives before consideration is given to the imposition of disciplinary measures.

9.2. Discipline and the role of the employer

9.2.1. It should be recognized that the employer has authority to discipline workers for employment-related misconduct associated with alcohol and drugs. However, counselling, treatment and rehabilitation should be preferred to disciplinary action. Should a worker fail to cooperate fully with the treatment programme, the employer may take disciplinary action as considered appropriate.

9.3. Elaboration and communication of disciplinary rules

9.3.1. In accordance with national law and practice, disciplinary rules concerning alcohol and drugs should be elaborated by the employer in consultation and cooperation with workers and their representatives. Such rules should be communicated to workers so that they clearly understand what is prohibited and the sanctions for violation of the rules.

9.3.2. Information, education and training programmes concerning alcohol and drugs should include work rules specifying the circumstances which could lead to disciplinary measures, including dismissal, as a result of alcohol- and drug-related problems.

10. Employment discrimination

10.1. Principle of non-discrimination

10.1.1. The employer should adopt the principle of non-discrimination in employment based on previous or current use of alcohol or drugs, in accordance with national laws and regulations.

10.1.2. Employers should maintain the confidentiality of all information disclosed by a job applicant or worker with respect to previous or current use of alcohol or drugs, in accordance with national laws and regulations.

Appendices

The development of an alcohol and drug programme for the workplace

A policy statement should outline the programme to be developed in the enterprise. It should take into account the social and cultural norms of the workforce, the environment in which it operates, the nature of the business, the geographical location (urban, rural), its accessibility to resources, etc.

The following elements are suggested for an alcohol and drug programme:

– *Coverage:* this programme should apply to all employees.

– *Timely intervention:* efforts should be made to ensure early identification and treatment of problems thus facilitating a good prognosis.

– *Participation:* participation in the programme should be voluntary without, however, denying management the prerogative of recommending employees for assistance. Participation should not prejudice an employee's job security or chances of promotion. The employee should not be disciplined or discharged as long as the individual participates in a rehabilitation programme and is deemed to be progressing towards an acceptable level of job performance. In this process, it is recognized that assistance under the programme should not permit a worker to disregard the normal responsibilities of employment. Failure to comply may result in discipline up to and including dismissal.

– *Confidentiality:* personal information on employees utilizing the programme should be treated in a confidential manner.

– *A balanced programme:* a balanced programme should include prevention, identification, treatment and rehabilitation components.

– *Training, education and communication:* the policy should include a programme on the prevention of alcohol- and drug-related problems in the workplace through information, education and training.

- *Referrals:* referrals may be made by the individual worker who considers that he or she may have a problem, by family members, by management or by a supervisor, colleague or workers' representative. The employer may refer the worker for medical examination or assessment by a qualified professional who will advise the worker if treatment is needed.

- *Reintegration:* this should describe the duties and responsibilities of the worker during and after treatment.

- *Programme review:* this activity should be undertaken at regular intervals. Information emanating from this exercise should be fed back into the design of the programme in order to increase its efficiency and acceptance in the workplace.

Linkages between alcohol and drugs and the workplace: A selection of studies

The scientific evidence linking the use of alcohol and drugs to negative consequences in the workplace and that linking working conditions to the use of alcohol and drugs is equivocal.[1] Some studies, however, indicate a linkage between alcohol, drugs and certain working conditions and between alcohol, drugs, and certain negative consequences in the workplace. The following lists are provided as guides. These lists are not exhaustive nor should they be taken to imply generally accepted conclusions.

Working conditions which may contribute to alcohol- and drug-related problems

Availability of alcohol or drugs at work, social pressure to drink or use of other drugs at work, travel/separation from normal social or sexual relationships, freedom from supervision, stress at work, precarious employment and the possibility of unemployment, monotonous work, shift work, night work or other work roles requiring relocation and associated with frequent changes in co-workers and supervisors.

Sources:

Ames, G.; Delaney, W.: "Minimization of workplace alcohol problems – The supervisor's role", in *Alcoholism: Clinical and Experimental Research* (Baltimore, Maryland), Vol. 16, No. 2, 1992, pp. 180-198.

---

[1] "Drug and alcohol testing in the workplace", Report of the ILO Interregional Tripartite Experts Meeting, 10-14 May 1993, Oslo (Hønefoss), Norway, (Geneva, ILO), p. 30.

Ames, G. M.: "Environmental factors can create a drinking culture at the worksite", in *Business and Health*, Dec. 1987, pp. 44-45.

—; Janes, C.: "A cultural approach to conceptualizing alcohol and the workplace", in *Alcohol, Health and Research World* (Rockville, Maryland, National Institute on Alcohol Abuse and Alcoholism), Vol. 16, No. 2, 1992, pp. 112-119.

Cherry, N.: "Neurobehavioral effects of solvents: The role of alcohol", in *Environmental Research*, No. 62, 1993, pp. 155-158.

Harris, M.; Fennel, M. L.: "A multivariate model of job stress and alcohol consumption", in *Sociological Quarterly*, No. 29, 1988, pp. 391-406.

House, J. S; Strecher, V.; Metzner, M.; Robbins, C.: "Occupational stress and health among men and women in the Tecumseth Community health study", in *Journal of Health and Social Behaviour*, No. 27, 1986, pp. 62-77.

Lundberg, I.; Gustavsson, A.; Högberg, M.; Nise, G.: "Diagnoses of alcohol abuse and other neuropsychiatric disorders among house painters compared with house carpenters", in *British Journal of Industrial Medicine*, No. 49, 1992, pp. 409-415.

Martin, J. K.; Blum, T. C.; Roman, P. M.: "Drinking to cope and self-medication: Characteristics of jobs in relation to workers' drinking behaviour", in *Journal of Organizational Behaviour*, No. 13, 1992, pp. 55-71.

—; Kraft, J. M.; Roman, P. M.: "Extent and impact of alcohol and drug use problems in the workplace: A review of the empirical evidence", in Macdonald, S., Roman, P. (eds.): *Drug testing in the workplace: Research advances in alcohol and drug problems*, Vol. 11 (New York, Plenum Press, 1994), pp. 3-31.

Mensch, B. S.; Kandel, D. B.: "Do job conditions influence the use of drugs?", in *Journal of Health and Social Behaviour*, No. 29, 1988, pp. 169-184.

Neale, D. J.: *Work-based alcohol risks in Alberta: An assessment* (Edmonton, Alberta Alcohol and Drug Abuse Commission, 1993).

O'Brien, O.; Dufficy, H.: "The nature of the problem", in Dickenson, F.: *Drink and drugs at work: The consuming problem* (London, Institute of Personnel Management, 1988), pp. 12-21.

Parker, D. A.; Harford, T. C.: "Gender-role attitudes, job competition and alcohol consumption among women and men", in *Alcoholism: Clinical and Experimental Research*, Vol. 16, No. 2, 1992, pp. 159-165.

—; Harford, T. C.: "The epidemiology of alcohol consumption and dependence across occupations in the United States", in *Alcohol, Health and Research World*, NIAAA, Vol. 16, No. 2, 1992, pp. 97-105.

Richman, J. A.: "Occupational stress, psychological vulnerability and alcohol-related problems over time in future physicians", in *Alcoholism: Clinical and Experimental Research*, Vol. 16, No. 2, 1992, pp. 166-171.

Seemann, M.; Seemann, A. J.: "Life strains, alienation, and drinking behavior", in *Alcoholism: Clinical and Experimental Research*, Vol. 16, No. 2, 1992, pp. 199-205.

Shehadeh, V.; Shain, M.: *Influence on wellness in the workplace: A multivariate approach*, Technical Report (Ottawa, Health and Welfare Canada, 1990).

Trice, H. M.: "Work-related risk factors associated with alcohol abuse", in *Alcohol, Health and Research World*, NIAAA, Vol. 16, No. 2, 1992, pp. 107-111.

—; Sonnenstuhl, W. J.: "On the construction of drinking norms in work organizations", in *Journal of Studies on Alcohol*, Vol. 51, No. 3, 1990.

WHO: *Health promotion in the workplace: Alcohol and drug abuse*, Report of a WHO Expert Committee, WHO Technical Report Series 833 (Geneva, 1993).

Alcohol and drug use and their negative consequences in the workplace

Adverse health consequences, increased absenteeism, deterioration in interpersonal relations, deterioration in job performance, lowered productivity, increased accidents, increased disciplinary problems, increased personnel turnover, training and recruitment costs, damage to the reputation of the enterprise.

Sources

Crouch, D. J.; Webb, D. O.; Peterson, L. V.; Buller, P. F.; Rollins, D. E.: "A critical evaluation of the Utah Power and Light Company's substance abuse program: Absenteeism, accidents, and costs", in Gust, S. W., Walsh, J. M. (eds.): *Drugs in the workplace: Research and evaluation data* (Rockville, Maryland, National Institute on Drug Abuse, 1989), pp. 169-193.

Crow, S. M.; Hartman, S. J.: "Drugs in the workplace: Overstating the problems and the cures", in *Journal of Drug Issues*, Vol. 22, No. 4, 1992, pp. 923-937.

Gutierrez-Fisac, J. L.: "Occupational accidents and alcohol consumption in Spain", in *International Journal of Epidemiology*, Vol. 21, No. 6, 1992, pp. 1114-1120.

Hanson, M.: "Overview of drug and alcohol testing in the workplace", in "Drug testing in the workplace", *Bulletin on Narcotics*, United Nations International Drug Control Programme, New York, Vol. XLV, No. 2, 1993, pp. 3-44.

Hingson, R. W., Lederman, R. I., Walsh, D. C.: "Employee drinking patterns and accidental injury: A study of four New England states", in *Journal of Studies on Alcohol*, No. 46, 1989, pp. 298-303.

Joeman, L. M.: *Alcohol consumption and sickness absence: An analysis of 1984 general household survey data*, Research Series No. 4 (London, Employment Department, Sep. 1992).

Idem: "Alcohol at work: The cost to employers", in *Employment Gazette*, Dec. 1991, pp. 669-680.

Kuhlman, J. J.; Levine, B.; Smith, M. L.; Hordinsky, J. R.: "Toxicological findings in Federal Aviation Administration general aviation accidents", in *Journal of Forensic Sciences*, No. 36, 1991, pp. 1121-1128.

Lehman, W. E. K.; Simpson, D. D.: "Employee substance use and on-the-job behaviors", in *Journal of Applied Psychology*, No. 77, 1992, pp. 309-321.

Lewis, R. J.; Cooper, S. P.: "Alcohol, other drugs, and fatal work-related injuries", in *Journal of Occupational Medicine*, No. 31, 1989, pp. 23-28.

Martin, J. K.; Kraft, J. M.; Roman, P. M.: "Extent and impact of alcohol and drug use problems in the workplace: A review of the empirical evidence", in Macdonald, S., Roman, P. (eds.): *Drug testing in the workplace: Research advances in alcohol and drug problems*, Vol. 11 (New York, Plenum Press, 1994), pp. 3-31.

Nakamura, K.; Tanaka, A.; Takano, T.: "The social cost of alcohol abuse in Japan", in *Journal of Studies on Alcohol*, No. 54, 1993, pp. 618-625.

National Transportation Safety Board: *Safety study: Fatigue, alcohol, other drugs, and medical factors in fatal-to-the-driver heavy truck crashes*, Vol. 1, NTSB/SS-90/01 (Washington, DC, 1990).

US Postal Service: *An empirical evaluation of pre-employment drug testing in the United States Postal Service, Final report*, Personnel Research and Development Branch, Office of Selection and Evaluation (Washington, DC, Dec. 1990).

Idem: *Utility analysis of pre-employment drug testing as a selection device*, Personnel Research and Development Branch, Office of Selection and Evaluation (Washington, DC, June 1991).

Zwerling, C.: "Current practice and experience in drug and alcohol testing in the workplace", in "Drug testing in the workplace", *Bulletin on Narcotics*, UNDCP, Vol. XLV, No. 2, 1993, pp. 155-196.

Effects of alcohol and drugs and indicators of potential problems

Physical effects of alcohol and drugs and indicators of potential problems

Studies have shown that the effects of alcohol upon the body vary on the individual because of the following factors:

(a) *Body size*. Persons who are larger than average, other things being equal, will not be affected as much as an average-sized person (70 kilograms for men, 55 kilograms for women) by the same amount of alcohol, while persons who are smaller than the average will be affected more.

(b) *Gender*. Women tend, on average, to be smaller physically than men and hence affected to a greater extent than men by the same amount of alcohol.

(c) *Rate of consumption*. The rate of consumption in a given period can greatly affect whether an individual becomes intoxicated.

(d) *Prior use*. Individuals who drink frequently will be less affected by a specific amount of alcohol than people who do not drink at all or very rarely, who will have less tolerance and therefore be affected more.

(e) *Time lapse between eating and alcohol consumption*. Alcohol will have a greater immediate physical effect on a person who has not eaten recently than upon someone who has, or who eats at the same time as consuming alcohol.

(f) *State of tiredness*. A person who is not adequately rested normally has a tendency to be more affected by alcohol consumption than one who is well rested; such a factor has obvious indications for workers on extended shifts or on those who work night shifts, perform physically strenuous work, or who for other reasons are short of sleep or physically tired.

Studies have also shown that the harmful effects of alcohol consumption, apart from clear intoxication, include post-alcoholic impairment which can manifest itself as follows:

(a) slow-down in reaction time;

(b) a deterioration of motor performance which can result in clumsy movements and poor coordination;

(c) deterioration in sight which can result in blurred vision;

(d) mood changes which can vary and result in aggressive behaviour and depression;

(e) loss of concentration which can affect ability to learn and remember information;

(f) a deterioration in intellectual performance, including a decreased ability to think logically.

Furthermore, studies have also shown that certain patterns of alcohol consumption can indicate the development of problems, the following being the most common warning signs:

(a) heavy drinking, indicated by a pattern of frequently drinking to change one's mood or to become intoxicated;

(b) drinking quickly, often gulping the first drinks;

(c) eating lightly, or skipping meals when drinking;

(d) expression of concern about drinking, by the person concerned or his or her family;

(e) intellectual impairment;

(f) accidents in which alcohol is involved;

(g) absenteeism or lateness to work due to drinking or its after-effects;

(h) most friends are heavy drinkers;

(i) most leisure activities involve drinking;

(j) frequent use of alcohol to relieve stress, anxiety or depression;

(k) the person concerned has attempted to reduce drinking with limited success.

In addition, studies point out that:

(a) Excessive consumption of alcoholic beverages can result in significant liver damage, and can otherwise be linked to or result in illnesses or body dysfunctions such as cancer, a stroke, deterioration in muscle strength, nerve-related dysfunctions for both men and women, and that any consumption of alcohol during pregnancy can be dangerous for the foetus.

(b) Alcohol consumption in combination with legal drugs – either those prescribed by a doctor or those available without prescription – or in combination with illegal drugs can have unpredictable effects, lead to medical complications and even cause death.

(c) Drinking immediately prior to commencing work or during meal breaks while at work can impair reaction time and have other adverse physical and psychological effects, thereby potentially leading to a hazardous situation or poor decision-making.

(d) Many drugs cause physical or psychological dependence, and may have side-effects and withdrawal symptoms.

(e) Consumption of different types of legal drugs which are not supervised by a medical doctor, or the combination of legal drug use with illegal drug use or alcohol, or the consumption of one or more types of illegal drugs only, can be dangerous, cause illness, and lead to adverse health consequences which might even result in death.

(f) Use of legal or illegal drugs immediately prior to commencing work or during meal breaks while at work can impair reaction time and have other adverse physical and psychological effects, thereby potentially leading to a hazardous situation or poor decision-making.

Examples of delivery mechanisms concerning alcohol and drug programmes in the workplace

Delivery mechanisms concerning alcohol and drug programmes in the workplace could include one or more of the following:

(a) integration of information, education and training programmes about alcohol and drugs into other activities, such as orientation or induction procedures following recruitment;

(b) use of posters, hand-outs, pamphlets and booklets concerning the enterprises's policy on alcohol and drugs;

(c) use of videos, films and other audiovisual material;

(d) seminars on alcohol- and drug-related problems in the workplace;

(e) coordination of delivery of information, education and training programmes concerning alcohol and drug policy in the enterprise with relevant community-based activities which may supplement or assist the employer and the workers and their representatives in their prevention activities.

Guiding principles on drug and alcohol testing in the workplace as adopted by the ILO Interregional Tripartite Experts Meeting on Drug and Alcohol Testing in the Workplace, 10-14 May 1993, Oslo (Hønefoss), Norway

Overview

Together, the social partners – employers, workers and their representatives, and governments – should assess the effect of drug and alcohol use in their workplaces. If they conclude that a problem significant enough to require action exists, they should jointly consider the range of appropriate responses in light of the ethical, legal and technical issues enumerated in this document.

A comprehensive policy to reduce the problems associated with alcohol and drug use may cover employee assistance, employee education, supervisory training, information and health promotion initiatives, and drug and alcohol testing. A workplace drug and alcohol testing programme is technically complex and should not be considered without careful examination of all the issues involved.

When a testing programme is being considered, a formal written policy should be developed indicating the purpose for testing, rules, regulations, rights and responsibilities of all the parties concerned. Drug and alcohol testing, as part of a comprehensive programme, should be based on the greatest possible consensus among the parties involved in order to ensure its value.

Background

Reliable analytical methods now exist to detect substances in breath and bodily fluids and tissues. These substances include alcohol as well as other drugs. To ensure programme success, the methods of detection to be used must be of the highest quality and reliability, taking into consideration the purpose of the test. Although the number of competent laboratories is growing, it is recognized that in many countries such facilities do not exist. Policies should therefore be developed to take this into account.

There are two categories of tests: screening and confirmation. The screening test constitutes a rapid but initial stage of the process. However, in the event of a positive test result, confirmatory methods should be used to verify the results. Some legally prescribed drugs may, under certain conditions, be misidentified as illicit substances. Under these conditions, a correct interpretation of the test results is imperative. This highlights the need for high standards not only in technical equipment but also in the training and qualifications of personnel.

It should be recognized that current methods of drug and alcohol testing may involve invasive procedures, which may constitute a risk as well as an intrusion into privacy. In addition, costs for a well-designed drug and alcohol testing programme vary and it is recognized that these may be considerable. It is therefore imperative that these issues be fully considered prior to implementation of any alcohol or drug testing programme.

Assessing the relationship of drug and alcohol use and the workplace

The assessment of problematic use[1] reflected in the workplace should recognize the inherent national, social, cultural, ethnic, religious and gender variables that will affect not only the mode and meaning of use but also the behavioural outcomes evidenced by use. The nature and significance of problematic use must be carefully evaluated.

It is also important to recognize that people often use multiple drugs. Those substances may include, but not be limited to, alcohol, prescribed or over-the-counter medications and illicit or controlled substances.

---

[1] If use of drugs and alcohol related to the workplace is found after assessment to cause a problem, then for purposes of this document it is considered to be "problematic use". In addressing the use of alcohol and drugs in the workplace, this document does not intend to encourage illegal behaviour.

In addition to the need for a sensitive instrument to assess problematic use of various substances as reflected in workplaces, the *significance* of those defined problems must be assessed. Is it a health, safety, disciplinary or other issue? The identified problematic use should be considered with respect to all of the relevant issues.

Effectiveness of drug testing

The scientific evidence linking the use of alcohol and drugs to negative consequences in the workplace is equivocal. Most evidence, so far, is anecdotal and inferential. Studies are lacking on whether testing programmes reduce possible work difficulties resulting from alcohol and drug use. The available data do not produce sufficient evidence to show that alcohol and drug testing programmes improve productivity and safety in the workplace.

Alcohol and drug testing only recognizes the use of a particular substance. It is not a valid indicator for the social or behavioural actions caused by alcohol and drug use. No adequate tests currently exist which can accurately assess the effect of alcohol and drug use on job performance. There are correlations between behavioural effects and blood alcohol concentrations, but there are variances among individuals. Such correlations have not yet been demonstrated for urine alcohol concentrations, blood drug concentrations or urine drug concentrations.

Programme outcomes

The manner in which organizational, local, national and international drug and alcohol policies and practices are mutually influential is poorly understood. The implementation of a successful policy in one country may have unintended consequences in other countries. Programmes which provide benefits in specific countries may have adverse consequences for other jurisdictions. Since the world is becoming more closely linked by the existence of multinational corporations and international trade agreements, for example, countries and enterprises should examine more closely the international impact of their initiatives. Drug and alcohol policies must be individualized to meet the needs of particular users. One locality's policy cannot meet all users' needs.

Concern about the consequences of drug and alcohol use in the workplace should be addressed in a comprehensive strategy. If testing is considered as one of the elements in a comprehensive strategy, the intended outcomes as well as unintended effects should be considered. Review of these effects can assist in the decision to include testing in a programme strategy or not. If testing is to be included, this review can assist in determining the nature and extent of the testing to be carried out.

Some of the intended outcomes may include:

–   Assistance in the development of a comprehensive programme to improve safety and security as well as to reduce potential legal liabilities.
–   A comprehensive productivity and quality assurance programme including reduction of absenteeism.

Some of the unintended outcomes may include:

–   Deterioration of the work environment through fear, mistrust, polarization between management and workers, lack of openness, and increased social control.
–   Not following legal and ethical rules.
–   Breaches of confidentiality.
–   Adverse effects on individuals as a result of errors in testing.
–   Decrease in security of employment.

Legal and ethical issues

There are ethical issues of fundamental importance in determining whether to test for drugs or alcohol. Is testing warranted? If so, under what circumstances? Recognizing that the situation differs in each country and each workplace, ethical issues are one of the most important concerns to be resolved before any testing is undertaken. Rights of workers to privacy and confidentiality, autonomy, fairness and the integrity of their bodies must be respected, in harmony with national and international laws and jurisprudence, norms and values. Workers who refuse to be tested should not be presumed to be drug or alcohol users.

The need for testing should be evaluated with regard to the nature of the jobs involved. With some jobs, the privacy issue may be determined to outweigh the need to test.

As a protection to workers, positive test results should be subject to independent medical review. For those workers whose positive test results reflect problematic drug or alcohol use, participation in a counselling, treatment or self-management programme should be encouraged and supported.

Various national laws, customs or practices may require that employees who test positive are referred for treatment, assigned to other work or that other means to ensure their security of employment are used.

Specific procedures should be developed which demonstrate a programme's capacity to comply with existing national laws and regulations. Such regulations may include:

– legislation on workplace drug and alcohol testing,
– labour law,
– medical confidentiality laws.

Drug and alcohol testing must be placed within the larger context of the moral and ethical issues of collective rights of society and enterprises, and of individual rights, as embodied in the Universal Declaration of Human Rights and international labour standards.

Other rights are also important: examples here are the right to choose one's own doctor, the right to representation if needed, the right to notification that testing will be carried out as part of a pre-employment screening programme, and the right to information on test results.

It is assumed that the participants in any work situation have rights and responsibilities which may have been agreed upon. Drug and alcohol testing programmes should fit within existing arrangements for ensuring the quality of work life, workers' rights, the safety and security of the workplace, and employers' rights and responsibilities (e.g. protection of the public interest).

Programme organizers should be sensitive to the potential for any adverse consequences of testing (e.g. harassment, unwarranted invasion of privacy). Workers should have the right to make informed decisions about whether or not to comply with requests for testing.

Safeguards should be installed to eliminate any potentially discriminating impact from testing. The testing programme should be conducted in a non-discriminatory manner in compliance with the appropriate legislation and regulations. In those jurisdictions with a constitutional right to work, efforts should be made to enable the person to remain in the workforce.

Programme organization and development

Setting up a programme

Where problems in workplace performance exist, a number of responses may be considered. If the problems are related to the effects of alcohol and drug use, the balance of the corrective strategy should lean towards education and prevention. Partners in the workplace must consider whether employee assistance programmes are available within the enterprise, through the trade union or external associations in the community at large.

Assistance programmes should be voluntary, "broad brush" approaches which are capable of addressing a wide range of health promotion issues. If drug testing is an option within the assistance programme, a number of methods exist including pre-employment, post-accident, reasonable suspicion, post-treatment, random or voluntary testing.

In any case, drug testing should be viewed only as part of a systematic approach which includes assessment, information on the effects of various levels of substance use, education concerning the elements of a healthy lifestyle and a programme of reintegration into the workplace for problematic drug or alcohol users.

The response selected must be directly related to the workplace problems to be addressed. The objectives to be met by the testing programme must be clearly defined and articulated. Before drug testing is selected as an appropriate response, there must be clear evidence that testing can reasonably be expected to achieve its intended goals.

In this context, it is especially important to determine that the technical capacity for state-of-the-art testing procedures exists and is used. Analysis of test results must take into account the differences between alcohol and other drugs.

Alcohol- and drug-related issues in the workplace

Programme policy statement

The written policy should detail the procedures to be adopted by the testing programme and these should be agreed upon by all the social partners. The policy should clearly identify the purpose of testing and the uses for the results. It should indicate any laws or regulations concerning drug and alcohol testing that may apply. If needed, a summary statement could explain how the programme intends to comply with those laws or regulations.

It should emphasize workers' rights, employers' rights, public rights and individual rights. It should identify the substances to be tested for and how these substances will be detected. It should describe the testing method and the relevance of that method to the results. It should explain the laboratory procedures and the analytical methods used by the laboratory. It should detail how the testing programme is to be organized, the level of administrative support required, the technical expertise needed, who will carry out the tests and with what equipment.

Any changes to the policy, because of new conditions or because other substances are being tested for, should only take place with the agreement of all the social partners.

Administrative structure

The testing programme's administrative structure, areas of responsibility and lines of authority should be clearly delineated in written form and should be made freely available. A specific organization officer should have primary responsibility for the programme's operations. The manner in which the testing programme fits within the organization's larger administrative structure should be clearly stated. The qualifications of programme personnel should also be clearly stated.

Administrative procedures should be established to ensure that procedures have been followed correctly. These procedures should address the status of the tested individual and the responsibility of the organization during the time that test results are being analysed.

Confidentiality

Standards to protect the privacy of the workers and to ensure the confidentiality of test results should be specified. Among these, the following guidelines should be observed:

1. The identity of the worker should be kept confidential.
2. The records concerning the worker should be kept in a secure location.
3. Separate authorization by the worker should be obtained before the release of each test result, specifying the tested substances.
4. Signed authorization to divulge information about a worker to third parties should name the specific individual(s) who will receive the information.
5. A separate authorization should be obtained for each intended recipient of information about the worker.
6. Authorization forms should be witnessed.
7. Policies concerning the confidentiality of the testing programme should be communicated to relevant parties.

Programme linkages

A mechanism should be in place for communicating test results to the tested person. Appropriate mechanisms should be established to allow that person to be referred for assistance when indicated and when the person consents.

Policy options/purposes

The purposes of any drug and alcohol testing programme should be specified in writing. Among the most common purposes given for testing programmes are:

–   investigations of accidents and incidents;
–   referral for assistance;
–   deterrence;

–   meeting legal and regulatory requirements;
–   communicating an organization's policy.

The form of drug and alcohol testing in a particular programme should be explicitly tied to the purposes of the programme. For example, many forms of testing may be adopted to meet regulatory requirements. Although there may be some disagreement regarding the value and utility of any particular form of testing, it seems that:

–   Reasonable suspicion and post-accident testing are most clearly linked to investigative purposes.
–   Pre-employment, post-treatment monitoring and voluntary testing may be most appropriate if the organization wishes to refer persons who have been identified as drug and alcohol users for assessment and consultation.
–   Pre-employment, random, transfer, promotional and routine scheduled testing may be compatible with deterrence purposes.

It is imperative to establish written criteria governing when to apply one of the options listed above. In addition, the frequency and duration of testing assigned as part of assistance monitoring and/or a return to work programme should be prescribed in the overall testing policy. When a pre-employment test is utilized, it may be part of a comprehensive medical examination used to determine fitness for work.

Determining which drugs to test for

Decision-making on testing should be flexible, and existing conclusions should be reviewed periodically. Decisions to test for alcohol and drugs should be made only when reliable and valid initial and confirmatory testing services or facilities are available. These facilities should protect confidentiality and, for forensic purposes, ensure the chain of custody. All positive results should be confirmed prior to notification or any other action.

Several criteria should be considered in selecting which substances to test for:

–   the prevalence rates and the consequences of use in the workplace;
–   the likelihood of harm to health due to use of various substances;
–   the likelihood of substance use affecting work-related behaviour.

Programme evaluation and review

Ongoing evaluation and review are essential to ensure that a testing programme is able to attain the objectives for which it was established. The plan for monitoring and evaluation should be set out when a testing programme is designed.

The evaluation plan should:

– be based upon the written goals and objectives established for the programme;

– identify means to determine whether or not the programme is being implemented as intended; and

– establish criteria and mechanisms for determining the impact and effect of the testing programme.

Evaluation plans should adhere to acceptable standards. Results of evaluations should be made available to all relevant parties.

Technical and scientific issues

In many parts of the world no programmes exist for the accreditation of testing laboratories. In order to ensure the highest accuracy and reliability of the testing programme, standard operating procedures should be in place to document the manner in which specimens are handled, instruments are checked for proper functioning and quality control is carried out. Accuracy and reliability must be assessed in the context of the total laboratory system. If the laboratory uses well-trained professional personnel who follow acceptable procedures, then the accuracy of results should be very high.

The working group recognizes that national and international standards are lacking. It recommends that the ILO consider using such standards as those developed by the National Institute on Drug Abuse and the College of American Pathologists as a basis for developing international standards.

Extreme caution must be exercised in the testing procedures. Testing specimens beyond the authorized list of drugs for other types of analysis (e.g. HIV, other disease criteria or pregnancy) should be expressly prohibited. Additionally, the possible impact of a positive result on an individual's livelihood or rights, together with the possibility of a legal challenge of the results, should set this type of testing apart from most clinical laboratory analysis. All workplace alcohol and drug testing should be considered as a special application of analytical forensic toxicology. That is, in addition to the application of appropriate analytical techniques, the specimens must be treated as evidence and all aspects of the testing procedure should be documented and available for examination.

The purpose for which testing is conducted will often dictate the specimen of choice. Typically blood is examined when impairment issues are addressed, while urine is examined when drug use is being questioned. In many countries the law may require consent prior to submitting to the sampling procedure. Before any sample is collected the employee should be informed as to the collection procedure, the drugs that will be tested for, the associated medical risk and the use of results. Provisions should be made for the protection of the personnel responsible for specimen collection.

At present, urine appears to be the best specimen for analysis in the context of detecting drug use in the workplace. Specimen collection procedures should be done in such a way that the privacy and confidentiality of the donor is protected as well as the integrity of the specimen.

Blood can be used to detect the presence of alcohol and most drugs. However, the invasiveness and discomfort of the sampling procedure, the requirements for a trained phlebotomist and provision for emergency medical assistance make blood a less desirable specimen for workplace testing.

In terms of testing for alcohol, the breath is the most commonly used specimen. Equipment is readily available and breath can be collected in a non-invasive manner.

At this time, insufficient data exist to support a recommendation for an alternative specimen such as hair, sweat or saliva.

Initial screening and confirmation methods must be based on different principles of analytical chemistry or different chromatographic separations.

Quality assurance and quality control protocols should be in place before the initiation of the analytical procedures. These procedures should encompass all aspects of the testing process, from specimen collection through reporting of the results to final disposition of the specimen. Quality assurance procedures should be designed, implemented and reviewed to monitor each step of the process.

A positive result does not automatically identify an individual as a drug user. The results should be reviewed, verified and interpreted by a medical expert. Prior to making a final decision, the medical expert would check all medical records, examine other medical explanations for a positive test result, and conduct a medical interview with the individual (including the individual's medical history). This would determine whether a confirmed positive result could be explained by the use of legally prescribed medication.

Before making the final interpretation of the test result, the individual should be given the opportunity to discuss the test results with the medical reviewer. If there is a legitimate medical explanation for the positive test, the result should be reported as negative and no further action should be taken.

Recommendations for action and research

The expert working group recommends that:

– Research should be undertaken to evaluate the relationship between use of drugs and alcohol and job safety and productivity.
– Research should be initiated to evaluate the costs and benefits of testing programmes. Evaluations should be done to study the costs and benefits for each of the parties, including social, economic and psychological costs and benefits.
– The ILO should consider the need for developing international standards for drug and alcohol testing and laboratory certification.

Selected bibliography of general and chapter-specific literature on alcohol- and drug-related issues in the workplace

General – Overviews, monographs and books

Brief, A. P.; Folger, R. G.: "The workplace and problem drinking as seen by two novices", in *Alcoholism: Clinical and Experimental Research*, Vol. 16, No. 2, 1992, pp. 190-198.

Blum, T. C.: "The presence and integration of drug abuse intervention in human resources management", in Walsh, J.; Gust, S. (eds.): *Drugs in the Workplace: Research and Evaluation Data*, NIDA Research Monograph 91, DHHH Publication ADM-89-1612 (Rockville, Maryland, Alcohol, Drug Abuse and Mental Health Administration, 1989), p. 245.

Butler, B.: *Alcohol and drugs and the workplace* (Toronto, Butterworth, 1993).

DeLancey, M. M.; Hannan, D. R.: *International guide to workplace substance-abuse prevention: A 16-country analysis of employers and employee rights and responsibilities regarding drug testing, treatment, and policy development, and overview of trends in drug and alcohol use* (Washington, DC, Institute for a Drug-Free Workplace, 1994).

Dietze, K.: *Alkohol und Arbeit* (Zürich, Orell Füssli Verlag, 1992).

Harford, T. C.; Parker, A. D.; Grant, B. F.; Dawson, D. A.: "Alcohol use and dependence among employed men and women in the United States in 1988", in *Alcoholism: Clinical and Experimental Research*, Vol. 16, No. 2, 1992, pp. 146-148.

ILO: *Drugs and alcohol in the maritime industry*, Report of the Interregional Meeting of Experts (Geneva, 1992).

Lenfers, H.: *Alkohol am Arbeitsplatz, Entscheidungshilfen für Führungskräfte* (Neuwied, Germany, Luchterhand Verlag 1993).

Mullahy, J.; Sindelair, J.: "Effects of alcohol on labor market success, income, earnings, labor supply, and occupation", in *Alcohol, Health and Research World*, NIAAA, Vol. 16, No. 2, 1992, pp. 134-139.

Normand, J.; Lempert, R. O.; O'Brien, C. P. (eds.): *Under the influence? Drugs and the American workforce*, National Research Council/Institute of Medicine, Commission on Behavioral and Social Sciences and Education, Committee on Drug Use in the Workplace (Washington, DC, National Academy Press, 1994).

Norwegian Ministry of Health and Social Affairs: *The negative social consequences of alcohol use* (Oslo, Aug. 1990).

Roman, P. M.; Blum, T. C.: "Life transitions, work and alcohol: An overview and preliminary data", in *Alcoholism: Clinical and Experimental Research*, Vol. 16, No. 2, 1992, pp. 149-158.

Russland, R.: *Das Suchtbuch für die Arbeitswelt*, Nr. 126 (Frankfurt-am-Main, Schriftenreihe der IG Metall, 1992).

Shahandeh, B.: "Drug and alcohol abuse in the workplace: Consequences and countermeasures", *International Labour Review*, Vol. 124, No. 2, Mar.-Apr. 1985, pp. 207-223.

Shain, M.: "My work makes me sick, evidence and health promotion implications", in *Health Promotion*, Winter 1990/91, pp. 11-12.

Smith, J. P.: *Alcohol and drugs in the workplace: Attitudes, policies and programmes in the European Community*, Report of the International Labour Office in collaboration with the Health and Safety Directorate, Commission of the European Communities (Geneva, 1993).

Trice, H. M.; Sonnenstuhl W. J.: "Drinking behaviour and risk factors related to the workplace: implications for research and prevention", in *Journal of Applied Behavioural Science*, Vol. 24, No. 4, 1988, pp. 327-346.

Wilsnack, R. W.; Wilsnack, S. C.: "Women, work, and alcohol: Failures of simple theories", in *Alcoholism: Clinical and Experimental Research*, Vol. 16, No. 2, 1992, pp. 172-179.

5. Restrictions on alcohol, legal and illegal drugs in the workplace

Osterberg, E.: "Current approaches to limit alcohol abuse and the negative consequences of use: A comparative overview of available options and an assessment of proven effectiveness", pp. 266-299, in Norwegian Ministry of Health and Social Affairs: *The negative social consequences of alcohol use* (Oslo, Aug. 1990).

6. Prevention through information, education and training programmes

Cook, R. F.; Youngblood, A.: "Preventing substance abuse as an integral part of worksite health promotion", in *Occupational Medicine*, Vol. 5, No. 4, Oct.-Dec. 1990, pp. 725-737.

Fauske, S.: *Design, implementation and management of alcohol and drug programmes at the workplace* (Geneva, ILO, 1992).

ILO: *Conditions of Work Digest*, Vol. 6, No. 1, "Alcohol and drugs" (Geneva, 1987).

Rohsenow, D. J.; Smith, R. E.; Johnson, S.: "Stress management training as a prevention program for heavy social drinkers: Cognitions, affect, drinking and individual differences", in *Addictive Behaviors*, No. 10, 1985, pp. 45-54.

Schneider, R.; Colan, N.; Googins, B.: "Supervisor training in employee assistance programs: Current practices and future directions", in *Employee Assistance Quarterly*, Vol. 6, No. 2, 1990, pp. 41-55.

7. Identification

Douglas, J. A.; Feld, D. E.; Asquith, N.: *Employment testing manual* (Boston, Massachusetts, Warren, Gorham and Lamont, 1989), with annual supplement.

ILO: *Conditions of Work Digest*, Vol. 12, No. 2, "Workers' privacy: Part III: Testing in the workplace" (Geneva, 1993).

Idem. *Drug and alcohol testing in the workplace*, Report of the Interregional Tripartite Experts Meeting, 10-14 May 1993, Oslo (Hønefoss), Norway (Geneva, 1993).

Macdonald, S.; Roman, P. (eds): *Drug testing in the workplace: Research advances in alcohol and drug problems*, Vol. 11 (New York, Plenum Press, 1994).

UNDCP: "Drug testing in the workplace", in *Bulletin on Narcotics*, Vol. XLV, No. 2, 1993. US Postal Service: *An empirical evaluation of preemployment drug testing in the United States Postal Service, Final report*, Personnel Research and Development Branch, Office of Selection and Evaluation (Washington, DC, Dec. 1990).

US Postal Service: *Utility analysis of pre-employment drug testing as a selection device*, Personnel Research and Development Branch, Office of Selection and Evaluation (Washington, DC, June 1991).

8. Assistance, treatment and rehabilitation programmes

Blum, T. C.; Martin, J. K.; Roman, P. M.: "A research note on EAP prevalence, components and utilization", in *Journal of Employee Assistance Research*, Vol. 1, No. 1, 1992, pp. 209-229.

—; Roman, P. M.: "Employee assistance programs and human resource management", in *Research in Personnel and Human Resource Management*, No. 7, 1989, pp. 259-312.

Foote, A.; Erfurt, J. C.: "Post-treatment follow-up, aftercare, and worksite re-entry of the recovering alcoholic employee", in Galanter, M. (ed.): *Recent developments in alcoholism*, Vol. 6, pp. 193-204 (New York, Plenum Press, 1988).

Guidelines to creating an employee assistance program (Toronto, Addiction Research Foundation, undated).

Harris, M.; Fennell, M.: "Perceptions of an employee assistance program and employees' willingness to participate", in *Journal of Applied Behavioral Science*, Vol. 24, No. 4, pp. 423-438.

ILO: *Conditions of Work Digest,* Vol. 6, No. 1, "Alcohol and drugs" (Geneva, 1987).

Kronson, M. E.: "Substance abuse coverage provided by employer medical plans", in *Monthly Labor Review*, Vol. 114, No. 4, Apr. 1991, pp. 3-10.

Ritson, B.: "Services available to deal with problems faced and created by alcohol users", in Norwegian Ministry of Health and Social Affairs: *The negative social consequences of alcohol use* (Oslo, Aug. 1990), pp. 227-259.

Roman, P. M.; Blum, T. C.: "Formal intervention in employee health: Comparisons of the nature and structure of employee assistance programs and health promotion programs", in *Social Science and Medicine*, No. 26, 1988, pp. 503-514.

Sonnenstuhl, W. J.: "Contrasting employee assistance, health promotion, and quality of work life programs and their effects on alcohol abuse and dependence", in *Journal of Applied Behavioral Science*, No. 24, 1988, pp. 347-363.

Steele, P. D.: "Substance abuse and the workplace, with special attention to employee assistance programs: An overview", in *Journal of Applied Behavioural Science*, Vol. 24, No. 4., 1988, pp. 315-325.

US Department of Labor: *What works: Workplaces without alcohol and other drugs* (Washington, DC, Oct. 1991).

9. Intervention and disciplinary procedures

Allsop, S.; Beaumont, P. B.: "Key legal issues: Dismissal for alcohol offenses", in *Employment Services*, 1983, pp. 28-32.

Bensted, A.: "The law and alcohol and drugs in the workplace", in Dickenson, F.: *Drink and drugs at work: The consuming problem* (London, Institute of Personnel Management, 1988), pp. 43-66.

Daintith, T.; Baldwin, R.: *Alcohol and drugs in the workplace: A review of laws and regulations in the Member States of the European Community* (London, Institute of Advanced Legal Studies, 1993).

Denenberg, T. S.; Denenberg, R. V.: *Alcohol and other drugs: Issues in arbitration* (Washington, DC, Bureau of National Affairs, 1991).

Industrial Relations Service: "Alcohol and drugs", in *Industrial Relations Legal Information Bulletin*, No. 315, Oct. 1986, pp. 2-8.

Industrial Relations Service: "Drink and drugs in the workplace", in *Industrial Relations Legal Information Bulletin*, No. 460, Nov. 1992, pp. 2-9.

10. Employment discrimination

Canadian Human Rights Commission: *Policy 88-1* (Ottawa, 1988).

Douglas, J. A.; Feld, D. E.; Asquith, N.: *Employment testing manual* (Boston, Massachusetts, Warren, Gorham and Lamont, 1989), pp. 12-26 to 12-39, and 1994 Supplement, pp. S12-60 to S12-65.

Equal Employment Opportunity Commission Technical Assistance Manual on the Employment Provisions of the Americans with Disabilities Act: Chapter VIII, "Drug and alcohol abuse" (Washington, DC, 1983).

Ontario Human Rights Commission: *Policy Statement on Drugs and Alcohol Testing* (Toronto, Nov. 1990).

Trubow, G.: *Privacy law and practice* (New York, Matthew Bender, 1991), pp. 9-18 to 9-21.